I1063928

Tiger Talk
All About Me

Keeping Well

Leon Read

SEA-TO-SEA
Mankato Collingwood London

Contents

Five a day   4

Brushing your teeth   6

Good exercise   8

Washing your hands   10

Feeling sick   12

Taking medicine   14

What a mess!   16

Bath time!   18

Time for bed   20

Feeling great   22

Word picture bank   24

Look for Tiger on the pages of this book. Sometimes he is hiding.

We can do many things to keep well.

Five a day

We need to eat a well-balanced diet.

This includes five fruits or vegetables a day.

Which foods do you eat?

stew and dumplings

pizza and fries

chicken and rice

pasta

Make your own favorite pretend food like this. →

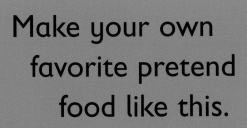

5

Brushing your teeth

We need to look after our teeth.

Brush your teeth twice a day
to keep them clean.

When was the last time you went to a dentist?

Good exercise

Exercise makes us strong.

We exercise by:

skipping...

dancing...

8

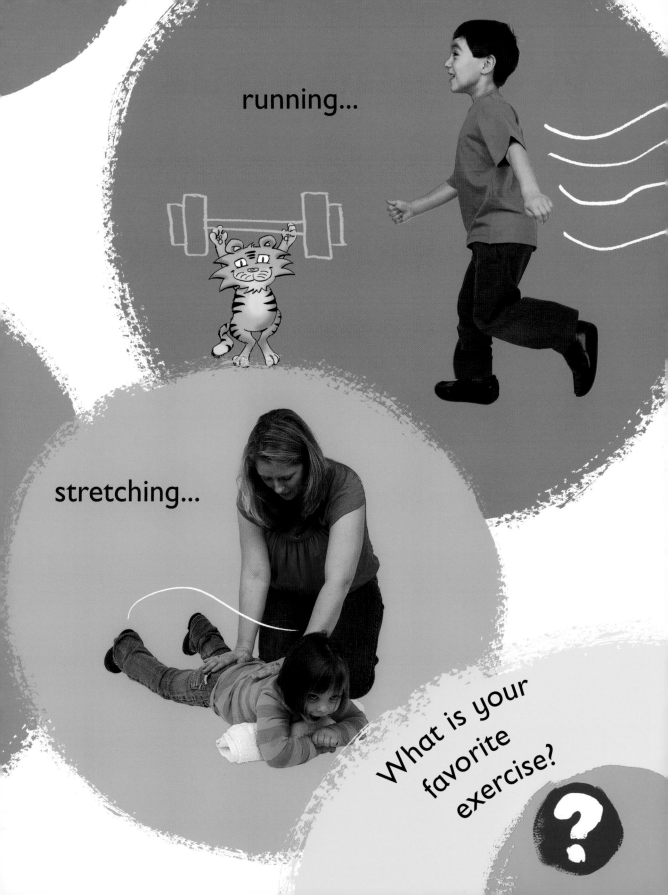

running...

stretching...

What is your favorite exercise?

Washing your hands

Before we eat, we wash our hands to get rid of dirt and germs.

11

Feeling sick

Germs can make us sick. Germs are tiny.
We can only see them using a machine.

a real germ

I'm making a picture of a germ.

Mom has taken me to the doctor because I am sick.

When was the last time you went to the doctor?

13

Taking your medicine

Sometimes we need medicine to make us better.

Tiger feels sick.

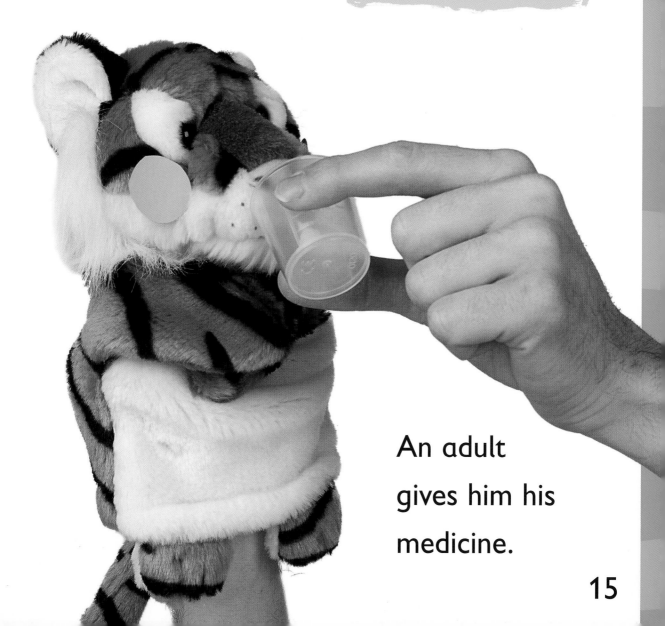

Only adults are allowed to give us our medicine.

An adult gives him his medicine.

15

What a mess!

Help keep things clean and tidy. Germs like a mess.

I help my dad clean up.

Look! Lucy has fallen down.

Why should Lucy tidy up her bedroom?

?

17

Bath time!

Imagine what would happen
if you did not wash.

You would stink!

We read a story
about a frog
who didn't
want to wash.

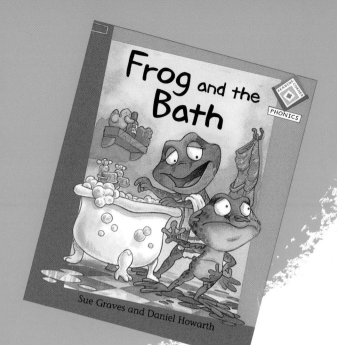

Frog and the Bath

Sue Graves and Daniel Howarth

What other ways can you keep clean?

Time for bed

Everyone needs sleep. Without sleep, we get tired and sick.

I like sleeping and dreaming.

What do you dream about when you sleep?

What time do you go to bed?

Feeling great

There are lots of different things we can do to keep well.

Adam is mixed up.

Help him remember how to keep well.

What do I
need to
do before I
eat food?

Why do I
need to
sleep?

Why do I
need to
exercise?

Why
do I need to
tidy my
bedroom?

Word picture bank

Dentist—P. 7

Doctor—P. 13

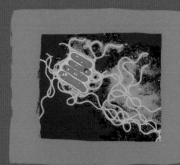

Germs—PP. 10, 12, 16

Pasta—P. 5

Skipping—P. 8

Wash—P. 19

This edition first published in 2010 by Sea-to-Sea Publications
Distributed by Black Rabbit Books
P.O. Box 3263, Mankato, Minnesota 56002
Copyright © Sea-to-Sea Publications 2010

Printed in USA

9 8 7 6 5 4 3 2

Published by arrangement with the Watts Publishing Group Ltd, London.

Library of Congress Cataloging-in-Publication Data
Read, Leon.
  Keeping well / Leon Read.
    p. cm. -- (Tiger talk. All about me)
  Includes index.
  ISBN 978-1-59771-186-9 (hardcover)
  1. Health--Juvenile literature. 2. Hygiene--Juvenile literature. I. Title.
RA777.R38 2010
613--dc22
                      2008045008

Series editor: Adrian Cole

Photographer: Andy Crawford (unless otherwise credited)
Design: Sphere Design Associates
Art director: Jonathan Hair
Consultants: Prue Goodwin and Karina Law

Acknowledgments:
The Publisher would like to thank Norrie Carr model agency
and Scope. "Tiger" puppet used with kind permission from
Ravensden PLC (www.ravensden.co.uk).
Tiger Talk logo drawn by Kevin Hopgood.

Dr. Linda Stannard/UCT/SPL (12tl, 24tr).
Katherine Fawssett/Image Bank/
Getty Images (19bc).

There are 18 Tigers, including me, in this book.
Did you find all of us?

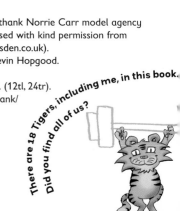